DECORATIONS CANDLES & WREATHS

DECORATIONS CANDLES & WREATHS

CHARTWELL
BOOKS, INC.

A QUANTUM BOOK

Published by Chartwell Books
A Division of Book Sales Inc
114 Northfield Avenue
Edison, New Jersey 08837
USA

Copyright © 1997 Quantum Books

ISBN 0-7858-0792-6

QUMCAW

This book was designed and produced by
Quantum Books Ltd
6 Blundell Street
London N7 9BH

Printed in China by Leefung-Asco
Printers Ltd

CONTENTS

DECORATIONS

Christmas is a special, magical celebration that helps to lift our spirits during the darkest time of the year. In almost every home the Christmas tree, with its ornaments and dazzling lights, becomes the focal point, creating a festive atmosphere that delights adults and children alike.

But shopping for decorations that suit your personal tastes and match your home decor is not an easy task, especially during the busy holiday season. It is much more rewarding to create your own special decorations. With the help of the

inspiring and inventive ideas presented in this book, you can decorate your Christmas tree in your own unique style. Have friends and family join in these projects to make Christmas a special time of quiet enjoyment and togetherness.

The projects in this book draw their inspiration from a rich variety of sources – from the traditional world of folk crafts to more elegant and exotic sources. The materials, too, are varied and interesting to work with. Metal foils, glittering glass beads, old bits of jewelry, and scraps of colorful fabric will add sparkle and shine to

your Christmas tree decorations. Sometimes, when working with flowers or shells, the natural beauty of the materials themselves will inspire the design. In other projects, some very ordinary household objects, such as scouring pads, are put to extraordinary uses with stunning results.

These festive Christmas tree decorations could become treasured additions to your family collection or lovely gifts with a personal touch.

MATERIALS

Many of the projects in this book have been inspired by the exciting and inventive work of folk artists from less technically sophisticated cultures than our own. The book aims to encourage the reader to be resourceful, to be inspired by everyday objects and to transform ordinary materials into lovely and unusual decorations. It is a good idea to build up a rich and varied collection of materials; to some extent the availability of materials will dictate your style and, therefore, how your work will look. Many of the materials in this book are quite readily available, either from a notions department, art suppliers or even your own collection of discarded items – nothing is more rewarding than recycling throw away objects into beautiful and useful things.

Hobby or bead shops have an amazing choice of products from all over the world, as well as wire and thread.

Once you have gathered together enough simple materials for a few of the projects, let your imagination loose and enjoy yourself, while discovering new ways of using materials and simple techniques.

METAL FOIL
The metal foil used for the repoussé work in the first six projects is really the only material that needs to be bought from a specialist source, such as a sheet metal supplier, although some may be available from good art or craft stores. Kitchen aluminum foil is much too thin, but if you do have difficulties finding the right metal foil, aluminum take-out or frozen fruit containers could be used. Another substitute is opened-up aluminum drinks cans – but always be careful when cutting metal and beware of sharp corners.

FABRIC AND RIBBONS
The fabric projects all use small scraps of rather vivid and lustrous materials saved from dressmaking, cut from old clothes or even found in a dress-up box.

The effect of appliquéd contrasting fabric with simple sequined and beaded embroidery is quite stunning, especially when crowned with brightly colored feathers plucked deftly from a feather duster (see the embroidered birds project on page 24).

Short lengths of exotic ribbon, brightly colored or luxuriant to the touch, can have stunning effects and are cheap to buy in very small quantities.

For the bird project (page 24), the sparkling stars project (page 26) and the luscious leaves project (page 28), small amounts of polyester padding were used to lightly stuff the decorations. You could also use nylon stockings or pantyhose.

BUTTONS AND BEADS

Nearly every household has some small tins and boxes, perhaps hidden at the back of a drawer, containing old buttons and beads. Supplement this collection with a variety of new buttons and beads of all shapes and sizes, including colored glass and plastic crystals, teardrop pearls, little seed beads and pressed metal charms. Always look out for exciting and unusual items when you are shopping, even if you are not making anything in particular at the time; you never know when you will need something really special.

JEWELS

Old or unwanted cheap jewelry is a good way of making a tree decoration look particularly exotic or resplendent. Look out for this in junk shops or at rummage sales; some good notions departments may sell flat-backed jewels. The little mirrors in the curly metal frames (page 20) come from a dolls' house shop.

PAPIER MÂCHÉ

Papier mâché pulp is a very versatile medium that was used to model the frosted fruit project (page 29), and the little painted animals (page 32). It has also been used as a backing for the dazzling dangles (page 42). It is widely available as a pulp mix from craft or toy stores, and is inexpensive when used in small quantities. You may even like to make your own pulp, especially if you enjoy working in this medium. The recipe is on page 29.

PAPERS AND WRAPPINGS

A wide variety of brightly colored papers, glittery candy wrappers, colored tissue paper and hand-printed Indian papers has been used in the découpage-inspired projects, ornaments galore (page 38). Build up your own supply by saving gift wrap, chocolate or Easter egg wrappers and anything else that catches your eye; it may be just what you will need some day.

NATURAL ITEMS

If you go for walks in woods, fields or along the beach, don't miss the chance to collect unusual items. Seeds, pine cones, shells, and poppy seed heads are all used in the projects on pages 48-50. Those you can't find, you can buy from specialty shops.

GLUES, PAINTS AND VARNISH

Four different types of glue are used in this book, and all are easily available – white glue, clear glue, epoxy glue and a cellulose paste for the decoupage projects.

The paints in the book are all acrylic or gouache. Both are water-based and both dry quickly to an opaque and water-fast finish. Polyurethane varnish is used on the salt-dough projects (page 54).

BASIC TECHNIQUES

All the projects provide guidelines and practical tips for creating stunning decorations. But this is only the beginning in each case there are endless possibilities to be explored. The aim of this book is to spark your creative talents and encourage you to experiment with other techniques and materials to invent your own personal designs.

No special technical ability is necessary for these projects, and they can all be made at home using simple everyday tools. Many projects use leftover materials such as candy wrappers and old newspapers that you might have saved.

1 For the sewing projects you can use scraps of fabric, ribbons, buttons, sequins, and brightly colored feathers plucked from a feather duster. You need only the most rudimentary sewing and embroidery skills. The success and quality of the decorations lies not so much in the skill of the maker but more in the clever and inventive use of materials.

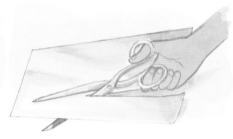

2 For some projects, particularly the repoussé metal decorations and the painted tin animals, you will need sheet metal foil from a good craft store or sheet metal supplier. These materials are surprisingly easy to work with. The metal is thin and cuts easily with scissors.

3 You can even draw on it, or trace designs from this book if you do not feel confident in your own drawing skills.

4 Papier-mâché pulp is used in several projects. You can use a ready-made paper pulp or make your own.

5 Some projects require simple craft techniques that most people have tried, such as découpage, painting, and modeling in papier-mâché.

6 Nimble fingers and a little patience are all that are needed for the simpler projects such as the pomanders. And what could be simpler than tying bows and stringing beads together?

CANDLES

The gentle, flickering, and friendly glow of candlelight has come to symbolize friendship and festivity. The intimate pool of golden light created as a focal point for a romantic dinner; the cluster of beeswax candles shining more brightly as daylight fades into dusk; the festive flickering of candles at holiday times – some of the most significant and memorable occasions in our lives are enhanced by the presence of candles.

In many parts of the world candles were the main source of artificial light until the comparatively recent advent of gas and electricity. From earliest times, candles and tapers were made by dipping rushes into tallow (an animal fat derived from sheep, pigs and cows), beeswax, or spermaceti (wax obtained from the sperm whale). It was only in the mid-nineteenth century that paraffin wax was first extracted from crude oil. The technique of molding candles, which now enables us to produce so many decorative and representational shapes, had been invented centuries before, in Paris in the fifteenth century.

or rolling a sheet of honeycomb beeswax around a length of wick, the enthusiastic amateur is encouraged to experiment with dyes and scented oils, with paints and applied decorations, and with imaginative displays.

The craft of candlemaking, with its long history and strong traditions, is one that offers creative opportunities to people with varying levels of artistic ability. After first experiencing the almost certain satisfaction of turning a colorless candle out of an improvised or ready-made mold

Successive sections in this book explain the basic materials and techniques you will need, then explore some of the delightful and unusual designs you can create by using rigid and flexible molds of all kinds. These decorations include deep purple candles scented with crushed lavender flowers, mosaic candles created from leftovers of colored wax, fish-shaped candles set in metal molds, and candles molded in bundt pans. Chunks of ice are used to create textured candles with a random series of holes, and cinnamon sticks are embedded in ice-blue candles for the most aromatic offerings ever.

The technique of rolling and molding

beeswax, so simple that it is literally child's play, fires the imagination for decorative ways to display the candles. Chubby, textured candles set in dough rings; slender dinner candles contrasted with bright shiny brass holders and glossy evergreens; hive-shaped candle domes embellished with insect shapes; harvest and Thanksgiving arrangements combining seasonal vegetables and honeycomb candles – there are plenty of

ideas for decorations the year around.

Decorating candles that you make or buy promises just as much craft satisfaction and at least as many decorative possibilities. You may want to embellish plain candles with studs or shells, buttons or beads, pressed flowers or spices; paint them with heavy texture or elegant shapes; or surround them with garlands of flowers and ribbons. Whatever your preference, you will find that you have more than enough choices.

MATERIALS

You can turn back the clock and produce effective and attractive candles with nothing more specialized than melted wax and a wick. But to increase your satisfaction in the craft, and the range and shape of your designs, you may want to experiment with molds, dyes, and a few other pieces of equipment. Your candle workshop could be an undisturbed corner of the kitchen or a gas burner on the patio. The illustrations show some of the equipment you will find helpful.

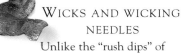

WICKS AND WICKING NEEDLES
Unlike the "rush dips" of Roman times, which were made of peeled rushes, present-day wicks are made of braided cotton chemically treated to improve its ability to burn. They are available in a range of thicknesses in round section (most suitable for use in beeswax candles and tall pillar candles) and flat section.

DECORATIONS
Pressed flowers and leaves, flat glass marbles, pearl buttons and beads, gold braid and whole spices – there is no end to the range of decorations you can add to or incorporate in your candle designs.

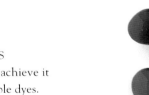

RIGID MOLDS

Ready-made molds in clear or opaque plastic and in metal come in a wide range of shapes and sizes. Choose from cylindrical or square, pyramid or cone-shaped, hexagonal and spherical molds. They all have a hole for the wick, and a firm base so that they will stand level.

WAXES

Uncolored paraffin wax is sold in various forms: as a large solid block, small cylinders, or easy-to-use flakes. Stearic acid, or stearin, used as a hardener, comes in small cylinders or flakes. Beeswax, an entirely natural product, is sold in block form to make molded candles of all kinds; the blocks are shades of untreated brown or bleached white. Beeswax is also sold in rolled sheets, in natural or dyed colors, to make hand-rolled candles.

CANDLE DYES

Think of a color and you can achieve it with the use of wax-soluble dyes. They are usually sold in the form of disks or "buds," which can be cut or scraped for use with small quantities of melted wax.

FLEXIBLE MOLDS

These are the ones you need for creating candles in a variety of representational shapes; for example, pieces of fruit, Christmas trees, pine cones and nursery-rhyme characters.

MAKING YOUR OWN CANDLES

A basket of fruit-shaped candles as appealing and colorful as any display of oranges and lemons, apples and pears; a school of pearly-white and deep-sea-blue candles set in oyster shells; a cluster of rolled honeycomb beeswax candles with their characteristic waffle-like texture and sweet, subtle aroma – in time you will surely want to make them all. But whichever candles you aspire to make first, you will achieve the best results by following a few simple, basic rules.

THE MATERIALS

At the heart of every candle is a wick, the means by which the liquid wax is carried to the flame. Choose the wick according to the size of candle you intend to make. Braided cotton wicks are sold in sizes described by the diameter of the candles for which they are best suited. For example, a half-inch wick is suitable for use with a candle that is half an inch in diameter.

Flat braided wicks are most commonly used, although round ones, which have a greater density, are recommended for use with beeswax candles and large, thick pillar candles.

Paraffin wax, an odorless wax that is a by-product of the oil refining process, is widely available, and because of its lack of color can be dyed to any required tint or shade, however light or dark. The wax is solid at normal room temperature, and melts between 135°F and 140°F. It is usual to add up to 10 percent stearin, or stearic acid, when using paraffin wax for candlemaking; in some cases the wax is sold already mixed with stearin, which both hardens the wax and slows down the burning rate. The addition of stearin is not recommended, however, when using flexible rubber molds because it tends to rot the surface.

Beeswax, too, both hardens the wax and increases the burning time.

Many church candles are made with a one-in-four proportion of beeswax and paraffin wax. A natural product of the hive, beeswax can be used alone to make long-lasting candles with a sweet scent. It is sold in block form, from which molded candles can be made, and, more commonly, in thinly rolled sheets. Cut to the required length and with a wick inserted, these beeswax sheets can be rolled in minutes to make the traditional highly textured honeycomb candles.

Although you can color wax with any wax-soluble substances such as poster paints and wax crayons, ready-made wax dyes are the easiest to control. They are sold in disk or bud form and are usually used in the proportion of ¼ ounce to 4½ pounds of wax. To use the dye in smaller quantities, or to dilute or intensify the

color, it is best to add it gradually to the melted wax and then allow a little to harden on a cold saucer. Only when it has set will you be able to judge the color of the finished candle.

MAKING MOLDED CANDLES

1 Lightly brush a flexible or rigid mold with clear vegetable oil (do not use extra virgin olive oil, which is cloudy) and blot any excess with some paper towel.

2 Thread the appropriate wick into a wicking needle and thread it through the hole in a rigid mold. Flexible molds do not normally have a prepared hole, so it will be necessary to pierce one.

3 Release the wick from the needle, allowing about an inch extra, and seal around the hole with mold seal or the tacky clay used by florists.

4 Suspend the wick vertically in the mold by tying it to a wick rod, a split cane, or a toothpick. Cut off excess wick and stand or balance the mold in an upright position.

5 Melt the wax in a double boiler or a bowl over a pan of simmering water. Stir in the

stearin, if you are using it, and any wax dye until it is evenly distributed.

6 Pour the melted wax into the mold and allow it to settle. When a well has formed around the wick, carefully top off with more melted wax and allow it to harden overnight.

   To release the candle from a rigid mold, invert it and give it a gentle tap. Carefully peel off a flexible mold, starting at the top and easing the mold gently all around the candle.

WREATHS

The craft of wreath-making is steeped in meaning and symbolism. Almost every ancient culture worshiped trees as symbols of divine energy. Evergreens, because they kept their leaves even through the dead of winter, were thought to possess special powers of eternal life. Branches of evergreens were exchanged as symbolic gifts conferring good health, and, to make the branches more decorative, they were bent around to form a wreath.

The wreath was also a form of head-dress. In fact, the word "crown" derives from the Latin word corona, meaning garland or wreath. The ancient Greeks crowned their champion athletes with wreaths of olive, laurel, and myrtle branches, which became symbols of triumph and excellence. During the Olympic games, the host city would

award wreaths made from local trees. The Romans, following in the Greek tradition, crowned their military and athletic heroes with garlands of oak and laurel leaves.

By the sixteenth century, Europeans had adopted the tradition of wearing wreaths in honor of religious holidays and to commemorate special events. For example, when a woman accepted the advances of a lover, she gave him a crown of birch; but if she rejected him, she gave him a crown of

hazel. Wreaths, whose circular shapes symbolize eternity, were considered fitting adornments at funerals.

Today, hanging a Christmas wreath on the front door is a well-established custom, but using wreaths to decorate our homes is a fairly recent innovation.

Decorative wreaths can be made with a wide variety of fresh flowers and foliage, or for long-lasting displays, from dried materials. Wreaths that incorporate useful items such as herbs and spices or gardening paraphernalia make practical as well as attractive gifts. The actual shape

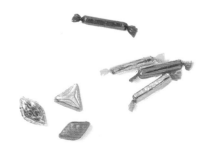

In this book you will find many inspiring ideas for creating your own wreaths. There are wreaths that celebrate the changing seasons; elegant formal wreaths; whimsical wreaths to delight young children; festive wreaths; functional wreaths that feature practical items; and, of course, wreaths that are purely decorative.

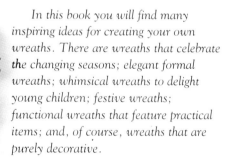

of the wreath does not have to conform to tradition; it can be square, oval or heart-shaped. Wreaths can also be used in innovative ways – to decorate the crown of a straw hat, as part of a bridesmaid's headdress, or as a table centerpiece. The options are limitless.

MATERIALS

WREATH BASES

The starting point for any wreath is the base, or frame. The type of base to use depends on whether the wreath materials are fresh or dry and on the size and weight of the finished wreath.

will show through and become part of the overall design.

2 Bases of florist's foam can be used with fresh or dried materials. They are easy to use; just push the plant stems into the foam until the base is completely covered.

3 Swag cage frames filled with blocks of florist's foam can be joined together into longer lengths for garlands and swags or made into circles for wreaths. Use these frames in the same way as foam bases.

4 Wire wreath frames are available in many sizes and when bound with damp sphagnum moss make a

substantial base for any fresh materials. The moss-clad frame can also be left to dry out to use with dried flowers.

5 Single wire rings make a good base for delicately shaped wreaths. They can be lightly padded with moss or simply bound with ribbon to complement the colors of the wreath decor. You can make your own wire rings or buy wire rings used for making lampshades.

1 Circles of twigs or vine, which can be bought or made from scratch, make useful bases for dried materials. If the base is not to be completely covered with material, it

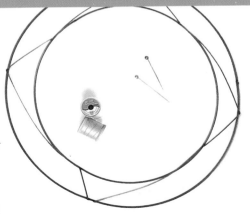

MOSS

Sphagnum moss is used to cover wire bases when making wreaths with fresh plant materials.

Soaking the moss in water for a few hours beforehand provides a damp base for insertion of the stems and helps to keep the finished wreath looking fresh.

Carpet or bun moss is much denser and greener than sphagnum moss and comes in flat pieces. Its rich velvety texture gives it a more decorative quality.

WIRES, TWINES & TAPES

There are many gauges of wire available for floral work, so you can match the thickness of wire to the materials you will be using.

Stub wires come in various lengths and are used for attaching fruits, cones and flowers to the wreath.

Reel wire comes on a continuous spool and is used for binding moss to a frame and other general uses. The finest reel wires can be used to bind together delicate materials such as brittle dried flowers or fine fresh flowers such as lilies-of-the-valley and grape hyacinths.

Garden twine is available in reels and balls and comes in green or brown. It is useful for binding the moss to a wreath frame and can also be used decoratively to tie materials together in small bundles.

Florist's tape is a rubber-coated tape used to cover the wires in the false stems of dried and fresh flowers.

GENERAL TOOLS

Florist's scissors are essential for cutting stems and can also be used to cut wires.

Pruning shears are needed to cut the woody stems on foliage.

An electric glue gun is a worthwhile, though not essential, investment. Heavy items such as nuts and pine cones can be fastened securely in place with hot glue, which sets in a matter of seconds. Choose general purpose glue sticks for wreath making.

A plant sprayer is useful for refreshing fresh flowers and foliage.

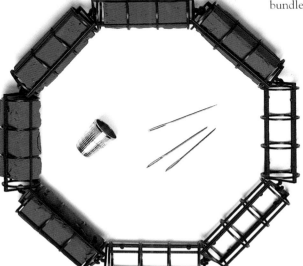

BASIC TECHNIQUES

MOSS BASES

Damp moss covering a wire frame is ideal for a wreath made with fresh plants. Wire frames can be bought from florists and nurseries and come in a variety of sizes, with either flat or angled sides. Remember that the finished wreath will be much fuller than the original ring when all the moss, foliage and decorative material has been added.

To make the moss base, soak sphagnum moss in water for several hours, then gently squeeze out the excess water. Open out the moss, place a handful on the top side of the wire frame and bind it on with reel wire or garden twine that has been twisted or tied around the frame to secure it. Continue adding moss and binding it in place until the frame is completely covered. Then secure the end of the wire or twine firmly to the frame.

For a more delicate frame, bend a wire coat hanger into a circle and pad it lightly with moss in the same way.

To retain their freshness as long as possible, keep the wreaths cool and spray with water every day.

VINE BASES

Vine or twig bases can be bought ready-made and are reasonably inexpensive. You can make your own using virtually any type of pliable twigs or vines, although wisteria, honeysuckle and grape are most commonly used.

If the vines are dry, soak them in water until they are flexible and easy to work with. Pick out a few stems and, holding them together, bend them around to form a ring of the required size. If the vines are too short, just add in other stems, staggering, twisting and overlapping the ends until they all hold together when bent into a ring.

Holding the vine circle in one hand, begin to wrap a long piece of vine around the ring, capturing shorter pieces as you go. For a vine base with more volume, add additional vines and wrap them in the same direction.

WIRING THE MATERIALS

Bunches of foliage, fruits and flowers need to be wired with stub wires before attaching them to wreath bases.

1 To attach soft fruits such as apples, limes and pomegranates to a wreath, push a stub wire through the fruit a quarter of the way up from its base, then twist the wire together, leaving one long end. Push another wire through the fruit at right angles to the first, twisting them together n the same way. Finally, twist the two long nds together.

2 To wire a pine cone, wrap a piece of stub wire around the base as close to the bottom and as far inside the cone as possible, leaving a long end sticking out.

3 To prepare nuts such as walnuts and brazil nuts, push a piece of stub wire into the eye of each nut and dot with glue to secure. For other types of nuts, wind the end of a stub wire to make a tiny flat loop, then glue it to the nut.

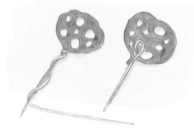

4 For a seed head with a stem, wrap the end of a piece of stub wire around the stem several times and leave a long end. For a seed head without a stem, glue a wire loop to the head.

5 Wiring flowers and leaves is necessary when the stems are delicate or if the flower heads are to be contoured or angled into a precise position. Wiring can strengthen the materials and make them much more pliable.

6 To wire a flower head, cut the stem to just a few inches long and push a stub wire horizontally through the base of the flower. Bend the pieces of wire down and twist them around the stem several times. Cut off one end, to leave a single wire stem, and cover the wire with florist's tape.

To wire a bow, tie it and push a stub wire through the back, twist the ends together and trim off any excess, leaving a long end to attach the bow to the wreath.

DECORATIONS

PRACTICAL PROJECTS

REPOUSSÉ METAL SHAPES

The stunning effect of these lovely glittering metal ornaments belies the simplicity of making them.

This lightweight metal foil is thin enough to be cut with an ordinary pair of scissors; the relief of repoussé work is created by drawing on the back of the metal with a dry ballpoint pen. You can use soft-drink cans if you cannot find any metal foil.

The metal foils used here are brass, copper, aluminum, and phosphorus bronze. Foils are very thin sheet metal. If you feel confident, draw the outline of your design directly onto the back of the metal with a soft pencil. Place the metal on a soft surface – an old magazine will do; now draw, pressing very heavily with a ballpoint pen over your pencil lines. Draw some freehand patterns – faces, stars, hearts, etc. – within the outline. Cut out the design with scissors and make a hole at the top for hanging.

Watch these metal shapes shine at night when the tree is all lit up.

LUMINOUS LEAVES

These lovely luminous metal leaves

accented with glass beads create a

beautiful shimmering effect

dangling from the branches

of the Christmas tree

like enormous

earrings.

Here are some precious-looking leaves to hang on your tree for a sparkling effect. Use the same types of metal foils that were used for the repoussé metal shapes described on pages 12-13. Cut some leaf shapes out of the metal foil and put them on a magazine. Make some leaf veins by pressing and rolling a tracing wheel across each one of the leaves.

Thread some brightly colored glass beads above and below the leaf with fine copper wire. The beads below the leaf help it to hang straight on the tree and contrast with the horizontal branches of pine needles.

A tree decorated solely with metal leaves, some with beads, some without, is a beautiful sight. The metal foil and beads sparkle in the reflected glow of electric Christmas tree lights.

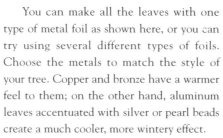

You can make all the leaves with one type of metal foil as shown here, or you can try using several different types of foils. Choose the metals to match the style of your tree. Copper and bronze have a warmer feel to them; on the other hand, aluminum leaves accentuated with silver or pearl beads create a much cooler, more wintery effect.

You might like to experiment by painting some of the metal leaves with transparent glass paints (see Metal Menagerie pages 16-17).

Make a lovely garland for your tree by stringing the metal leaves together on a thin copper wire and interspersing them with glass beads.

These

shiny

metal leaves

make stunning

tree decorations.

Luminous leaves

can be made in a

great variety of

shapes and sizes

from several types

of metal foils.

METAL MENAGERIE

These charming little animals made from copper or aluminum foil are

inspired by the popular tin decorations from Mexico.

Transparent glass

paints can give an

extra sheen to a

colorful metal

menagerie.

Cut out simple animal shapes and draw patterns on the back with a ballpoint pen.

Transparent glass paints can be used to good advantage on these metal figures; the metal sheen glimmering through the paint is very arresting. When the paint is thoroughly dry, you could try lightly rubbing the raised drawn lines with very fine sandpaper to reveal the glinting metal beneath.

The cornucopia, fish, and vase with flowers were made the same way and painted with opaque enamel paints. Matte or shiny paint can be used.

There are endless possibilities for

these decorations; visit museums

and galleries or look in art and craft

books for inspiration.

HEAVENLY SHAPES

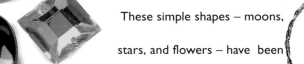

These simple shapes – moons, stars, and flowers – have been cut out of aluminum, bronze, and copper foil. There is very little repoussé work on the back; the glittering effect is created by adding flat-backed "jewels."

The crescent moon was edged from the back of the foil with a tracing wheel to create an even line of little raised dots on the front. Brightly colored "jewels" with different-sized facets were added to create a regal feel. Most clear adhesives are strong enough to hold the "jewels" in place.

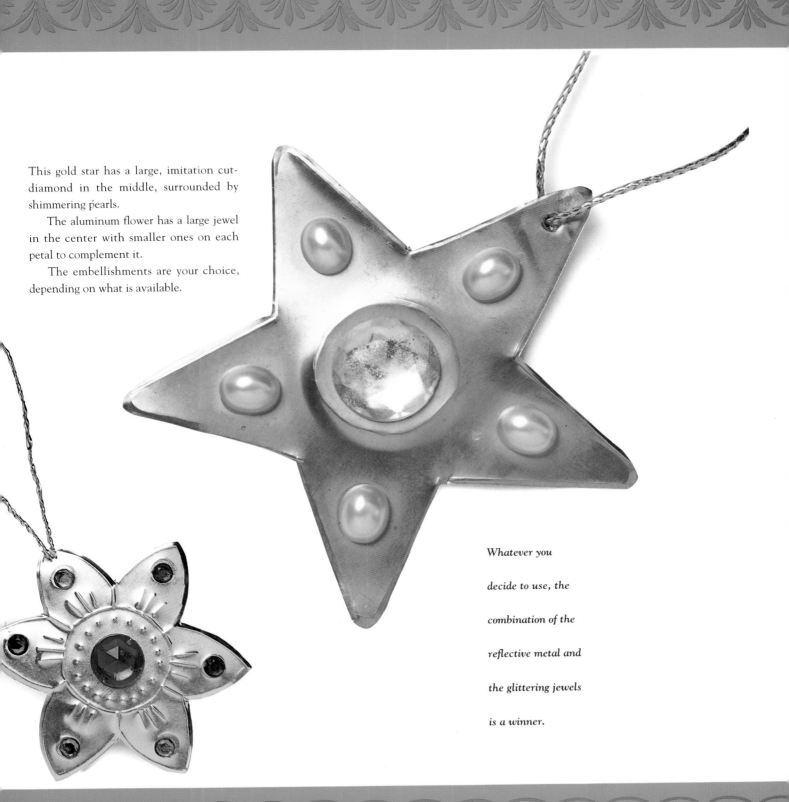

This gold star has a large, imitation cut-diamond in the middle, surrounded by shimmering pearls.

The aluminum flower has a large jewel in the center with smaller ones on each petal to complement it.

The embellishments are your choice, depending on what is available.

Whatever you

decide to use, the

combination of the

reflective metal and

the glittering jewels

is a winner.

MINIATURE MIRRORS & JEWELS

These miniature framed mirrors are inspired by Indian embroidery, in which lots of tiny mirrors are sewn onto a piece of fabric to give it a wonderfully rich and sparkling texture.

Cut the mirror frames out of the metal foil and draw some repoussé designs on the back, perhaps to frame the mirror or decorate the hanging tab.

The curly effect is produced by simply cutting the metal frame into very thin strips all around the outside. If the strips are cut thin enough, the metal will automatically curl into this unusual border. Stick your mirror onto the center of the frame with a strong epoxy glue. You can find small round, oval or rectangular mirrors where doll house miniatures are sold. Glue some little seed pearls or glass beads around the mirror to disguise the mirror's edge.

You may prefer to have a large jewel in the center of the frame instead of a mirror.

Try hanging these miniature mirrors on your lighted tree. Turn off the room lights and watch the mirrors throw their magical reflections around the darkened room.

The tiny mirrors in the center of these decorations add radiance and sparkle to any Christmas tree.

Metal figures can be used in several ways – as wreath decorations, crib figures, gift tags, and, of course, Christmas tree ornaments.

METAL FIGURES

The man on the right and the woman on the

opposite page are roughly based on images of

seventeenth-century Pilgrims who founded the

colony at Plymouth, Massachusetts.

You can really go to town working on the back of these metal figures with a dry ballpoint pen. Don't forget to pierce a hole in the top for suspending the little figures from the tree.

Why not make a whole family and their animals? What about Noah and his Ark? Or a nativity scene? The little angel at left could be one of your crib figures.

Metal figures look lovely pinned onto the front door at Christmas or perhaps attached to a festive wreath. Smaller figures could be made as gift tags, with the name of the recipient on each one. Remember you must write backwards so that the words will read correctly from the front.

This sturdy

little

character

was given lots of

interesting features

by drawing on the

back with a

ballpoint pen.

EMBROIDERED BIRDS

What is more appropriate than to have a flock of birds settle on a tree? Perhaps these visitors have come from more exotic lands to brighten up our winters.

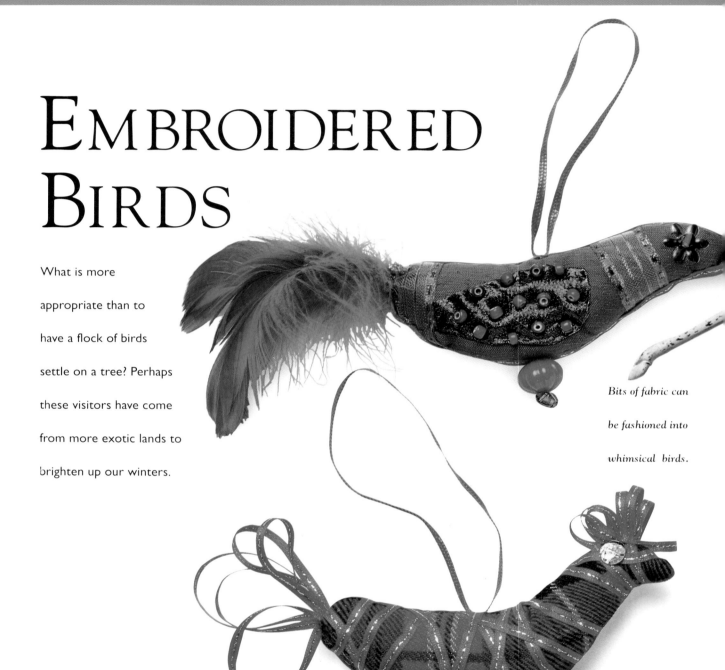

Bits of fabric can be fashioned into whimsical birds.

These unusual little birds, made from scraps of fabric and glittering ribbons, are embroidered with small seed beads and shining sequins. Little assorted packages of colorful sequins are readily available in most notions departments.

Use small pieces of fabric: the more exotic the better. Try gold lamé, shot silk, or diaphanous lace. Draw a very simple bird-shaped body onto a double thickness of fabric and cut it out slightly larger, taking the seam into account. Sew the pieces together, right sides facing, and leave a small opening for the padding. Turn right side out, fill with padding, and sew up the hole. Appliqué small contrasting bits of fabric for the wings, then embroider with beads and sequins. Add some ribbons. For the tails, you can use brightly colored feathers from feather dusters. Always make sure the eyes stand out.

The Scottish tartan bird with rhinestone eyes has a crown and tail made from the thin red ribbon that binds the body.

Gold tassels, small bells or a rich combination of beads hanging under the bird make an interesting addition.

The star and these little parcels are made from colorful fabrics and then embellished with bright ribbons and sequins.

SPARKLING STARS & PRECIOUS PARCELS

Stars hold a very special significance at Christmas. It was a gleaming star that led the Three Kings from far-off lands to the humble stable in Bethlehem. Stars hanging on our Christmas tree remind us of the star of Bethlehem.

These sparkling stars and precious little parcels are very easy to sew. Just cut out a star or parcel shape from a double thickness of fabric, remembering to add the seam allowance. Choose a variety of fabrics, perhaps ones that are richly patterned or have an antique look. You could also try shimmering and tinsel-like fabrics.

With the fabric right sides together, neatly sew around the shape, leaving a small opening. Turn the fabric right side out and stuff loosely. Insert a hanging loop before sewing up the opening.

Then go to town on the decorations, adding sequins and beads. Tie the parcels with colorful ribbons and bows. Cross the star with narrow ribbons and stud with starry sequins. Perhaps you could even add little jingle bells to each point of the star. Try hanging tassels from the three lower points of the star.

Tassels are easy to make. Simply wrap a small skein of metallic thread around your fingers, remove, and bind one end of the skein with the same thread. Cut the other end to form the tassel.

These delightful ornaments are easy to make; all you need is some fabric and glitter and lots of imagination.

This richly patterned red star with its shiny gold tassels would be a lovely feature on your Christmas tree.

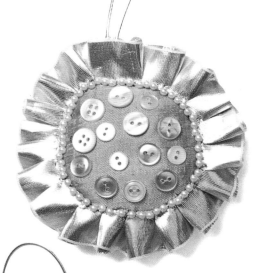

LUSCIOUS LEAVES & FLOWERS

These leaves and flowers are very easy to make and are so effective as Christmas ornaments. The pearly flower is made like a little cushion with a pleated silver ribbon edge. The gray silk center of the flower was decorated with a collection of old and new pearl buttons to signify seeds and then circled with a twinkling row of tiny pearls.

Use rich dark velvet to make the leaves. Cut a double layer of fabric into simple leaf shapes; be sure to include the seam allowances. Try using a contrasting color for the back of the leaf. With the right sides of the fabric facing together, sew around the leaf, leaving one end open. Turn right side out, stuff loosely, and, after inserting a hanging loop, sew up the open end. Use metallic thread to embroider the front with leaf veins. Pinpoint the ends of the veins with little seed pearls. As a variation, use long silvery beads to accentuate the leaf motif and finish with tiny iridescent seed beads. Finally, bind the hanging end of the leaves with matching metallic thread.

FROSTED FRUITS

These fruits
were modeled
in papier-mâché
and allowed to dry thoroughly before
being primed with a thick white primer
and painted rich, ripe fruit colors. When
the paint was dry, a little gold powder was
dusted over the surface.

Those lovely tendrils on the grapes are
easy to make from copper foil, which curls
naturally when cut into thin strips.

Although ready-made pulp is available
from craft or better toy stores, you may
enjoy making your own from this recipe.

Tear a newspaper into small squares
and, in an old pan, boil in plenty of water
until the paper begins to disintegrate. Let
cool, then mash with a potato masher.
Drain off excess water and squeeze dry.
Add half a cup of white glue, a sprinkling
of dry wallpaper paste, half a cup of plas-
ter-based filler and one cup of fine saw-
dust. Knead energetically until all the
ingredients are well mixed. This pulp mixture will keep covered for a number of
weeks in the refrigerator.

These little gold-dusted fruits are

modeled out of papier-mâché pulp;

the leaves are made from copper

foil, which is pushed into the pulp

fruit while it is still soft.

You could make a

variety of fruit and

create a riot of

shimmering colors

to decorate

your tree.

Try putting a little rider or acrobat on the horse, or make a sleigh for the reindeer to pull.

LITTLE PAINTED ANIMALS

These charming little animals are inspired by carved and

painted wooden toys made in India.

Start by making an internal framework of pipe cleaners and attach it to a cardboard base with strong glue. Model papier-mâché pulp (see page 29) around the framework to create an animal form – a horse, a fox, or a reindeer. Insert a little loop of wire into the back of the animal and cover the base with pasted newspaper strips. After it is thoroughly dry and primed, paint the animals in the manner of naive folk art, sometimes leaving the white primer to show as a contrast to the bright color. Add patterns, dots, and stripes, using colors that clash or dazzle.

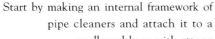

Engraving on

painted ornaments

produces some

intriguing designs

with a very

professional look.

Engraved ornaments are a real pleasure to make. First wrap Styrofoam® balls with two layers of pasted paper. Let dry, then prime with two coats of white primer. Push a chopstick into one end of the ball to provide a handle and then start painting the ball with some brightly colored designs. When you remove the stick, the hole can be filled with glue to hold the hanging loop, which is a piece of gold pipe cleaner threaded with a bright glass bead.

When the paint is dry, add some finer details to your designs by carefully scratching out a pattern to reveal the white primer beneath the paint. Use a sharp pointed instrument, such as the blade of a mat-knife.

This engraving process is a traditional technique used in Switzerland to decorate Easter eggs. As you can see from the balls shown here, the final effect is very attractive and professional looking. People are always intrigued with these engraved ornaments and want to know how they were made.

PAINTED & ENGRAVED ORNAMENTS

These painted and engraved baubles make a spirited change from the traditional

glass balls that usually hang on the Christmas tree.

Save your Christmas gift wrapping paper and use it to make next year's ornaments. This is one of the quickest and most rewarding projects in the book.

ORNAMENTS GALORE

The continuous surface of a

sphere provides an enormous

canvas for decorating ideas.

There is no end to

the variety of

attractive

ornaments you can

make using odd bits

of paper and some

glittery

embellishments.

To make these colorful and decorative ornaments, first paper some Styrofoam® balls with an array of different background colors. Then, using old bits of wrapping paper, candy wrappers, sequins, pearl-headed pins, glitter, some metallic thread and lots of imagination, make a whole range of dazzling ornaments. You could try some of the various techniques used to make the ornaments shown here. Dot the ball with flower-shaped sequins, securing them with small pearl-headed pins. Découpage motifs can be cut out of beautiful hand-printed papers. To add glittering silver stars; first paint some glue stars on the ball and then sprinkle them with glitter. Foil candy wrappers cut into strips are ideal for creating glittering striped balls. Bits of torn-up shiny paper can be glued between the stripes for added interest. Try binding some metallic thread over natural handmade papers or over crushed colored tissue paper.

MINIATURE CHURCH & HOUSES

These are buildings straight out of a fairy tale. Try making a whole village or the witch's cottage from the story of Hansel and Gretel.

These buildings are very simple to assemble from thin pieces of cardboard. The ones shown here were made from pizza boxes.

Look for ideas and inspiration in magazines, picture books, and especially travel catalogs. Make a simple house shape by sticking the cardboard together with white glue; use small strips of masking tape to hold the cardboard pieces in place while the glue dries, then paste thin paper all over the little building. Allow it to dry, then prime and paint with bright colors. Add sequins, glitter, and fine braid to finish.

This miniature church and the quaint little houses are modeled on decorative buildings of Eastern Europe.

DAZZLING DANGLES

These dazzling

dangles are

modeled out of

papier-mâché.

The glittering

jewels in the

center are added

while the pulp

base is still soft

and moist.

Model some stars, crescents, diamonds, hearts, and circles from papier-mâché pulp. While they are still soft, push a large, flat-backed faceted jewel into the center of each shape. The paper pulp will conveniently shrink a little when drying and hold the jewel firmly in place.

You can use any type of costume jewelry to make these dangles. This would be a good use for those old pieces of costume jewelry that you no longer wear. Anything that glitters will make a lovely center-piece for your ornaments.

Broken antique blue and white china shards can also be used instead of jewels. The dangles shown here were made with bits of eighteenth-century English china. The eccentric shape of the shard will dictate the way the pulp is modeled around it.

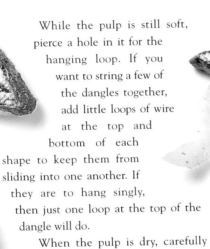

While the pulp is still soft, pierce a hole in it for the hanging loop. If you want to string a few of the dangles together, add little loops of wire at the top and bottom of each shape to keep them from sliding into one another. If they are to hang singly, then just one loop at the top of the dangle will do.

When the pulp is dry, carefully paint around the china or jewel with gold paint. For a really lustrous effect, add precious-metal leaf on top. You can buy books of silver, gold, copper, aluminum, or even patinated metal leaf quite inexpensively. It sticks readily to varnish that is just tacky and nearly dry. The final effect can be quite stunning.

Using odd bits of broken china adds interesting textures and shapes.

BEADS, BELLS, & BOWS

These stylish, elegant decorations are quick and

simple to make, but you need to be bold and

extravagant.

Use large beads and chandelier-type drop crystals for these tree ornaments. The ones shown here are made with a combination of large Indian pressed-metal beads and imitation crystals, which come in a range of colors and are much less expensive than glass crystals.

Figure out your color scheme carefully, perhaps adding little glass beads of a contrasting color between the crystal and metal beads. It is best to use thin copper or silver wire for threading; this is available in craft or bead shops. Complete your decorations with an elegant flourish, such as a matching bow at the top of the beads.

RADIANT RINGS

Decorative hoops

embellished with

beads and bows,

are an interesting

variation on hanging glass beads.

You can buy hoops or wire rings from jewelry suppliers or bead shops, or simply make your own from silver wire. Hang a combination of pressed metal and glittering glass beads from the bottom of the ring.

To make the ribbon rings, first pad the wire ring with polyester, creating some thickness, then tightly wrapping it with ribbon.

The ribbon ring on the right was finished with a pink organdy bow that picks up the iridescence in the crystal beads. The other two rings have gleaming gold bows to accent their blue and gold theme.

You could also try

threading beads

onto the wire ring

as shown below.

LARGE BEADED TASSELS

This golden tassel

was designed for a

large, boldly

decorated

Christmas tree.

Gold tassels have an opulent and palatial feel

about them, and these simple beaded tassels

have a glorious effect. Yet, both are deceptively

simple to make.

Try making a more unusual tassel, like the one shown opposite in gauzy lilac organdy. It is tightly bound at the top with gold thread, and threaded above with gold beads. A beautiful bronze ruched ribbon, tipped with a modest lilac bow, gives an elegant finishing touch.

The large tassel shown on the left is suspended from a gold-sprayed ball flecked with gold leaf. A rosette of metallic woven ribbon tops it off beautifully.

SHELL ORNAMENTS

The natural world is full of inspiration for the artist. What object could have more exquisite perfection and beauty than a seashell, with its extraordinary spiral forms and the natural iridescence of its pearly surface? The tree ornaments shown on these pages use teardrop pearls, beads, and ribbons to accentuate the natural beauty and charm of seashells.

Seashell ornaments

shimmer in the

light.

Shell ornaments are ideal for the sophisticated tree with pale, subtle colors. Use them with white, silver, or pearly decorations, and your tree will take on an otherworldly quality.

Collect interesting shells from the beach or buy them in gift or specialty shell shops (they are generally inexpensive). If you buy shells, choose common varieties that are not endangered.

Seashells are quite soft, so it is easy to drill little holes into them with a small awl or drill. Suspend teardrop pearls, silver stars, crystals, silver lockets, or little bunches of bells from silver wire threaded through the holes. Use ruched ribbons or polka-dot netting to complete the decoration.

NUTS & SEEDS

Nuts,

pine cones,

seed heads, and

cinnamon sticks

make naturally

beautiful

ornaments.

The incredible world of nature offers a wealth of

intricate design. Walnuts, which are of course

already designed to hang from a tree, are even

more beautiful when sprayed gold or silver.

To embellish the natural design of nuts and seed heads, hang little metal charms beneath them. You could also quarter a walnut with shining red braid and top it with a matching plume of brightly colored feathers for a whimsical touch.

Alternatively, cut a walnut in half, scoop out the nut, and line the inside with luscious fabric. Then glue a gleaming jewel in the center and little seed pearls around the edge to accent the natural heart shape. Hang the nut shell from the tree with red braid attached with a little bow.

Spray a pine cone gold and top it with a gold bow and hanging loop. Or you could try painting the cones red or green and then adding glitter to the tips. Finish them with little tartan ribbon rosettes and matching braid hanging loops.

A poppy seed head makes an ideal Christmas tree ornament. Spray it gold, then pierce a little hole in the stem and fill it with glue. Insert a hanging loop that has been threaded with one or two glistening glass beads.

A little bunch of cinnamon sticks tied together with gold braid and a tassel is very evocative of the winter season.

When out on country walks, look for interesting nuts and seeds that you could use for tree decorations. With an inventive mind and creative combinations, the variety of ornaments you can make is limitless.

A cinnamon stick ornament gives off a delicious scent.

POMANDERS

Everybody knows of the Elizabethan pomander – an orange,

preserved and studded with spicily scented cloves. But there are

many alternatives to this old favorite.

Some are very simple to make,

and they are all quite

lovely.

These pomanders

could be scented

with a spicy

Christmas pot-

pourri essence.

For the shell pomander, quarter a Styrofoam® ball with gold ribbon and attach the tiny seashells with white glue inside each quarter. To help keep the shells in place while the glue is drying, make a little fence of dressmaking pins around the inside edge of the ribbon that defines the quarter you are working on. For neatness, attach all the shells in one direction. When the ball is completely covered, make a rosette with the same type of ribbon, then push the rosette and a hanging loop into a small glue-filled hole at the top of the pomander.

The rosebud and white helicrysum pomanders couldn't be simpler. Just push the pointed dried flower stems into a foam ball.

SALT DOUGH

Salt dough is another traditional favorite for
Christmas decorations. And it is
particularly suitable for children, as
long as they don't try to eat it!

Salt-dough

ornaments can

be left in their

natural state or

painted with

vibrant colors.

The basic recipe for salt dough is 2 cups of all-purpose flour and 1 cup of salt. Add water gradually to the dry ingredients until the mixture is stiff, but not sticky, then knead for about ten minutes until it is smooth and manageable.

Working on a floured board, shape wreaths, hearts and baskets of flowers out of the dough. Use bits of dough to add interesting details and embellishments. Make a hole through the top of the dough figure for threading a ribbon, or just glue the ribbon onto the back.

When you have made your shapes, allow them to dry thoroughly for a few days. A warm oven may help for a short time, but take care not to cook them or they will yellow.

Varnish some of the shapes in their natural color. Paint others with vivid colors to look like South American salt-dough decorations. Varnish these as well to enhance the color.

GARLANDS

Garlands provide a wonderful contrast to vertically hung

decorations. A tree lavishly swagged and

looped with glorious garlands is a spectacle

to behold. Here are some ideas to spark

your imagination.

Garlands can be

made with everyday

objects such as

scouring pads and

packing chips.

Gold and silver

paint or sequins

produce some

stunning effects.

Golden ribbons and

glass beads create

an exquisite-looking

garland for your

Christmas tree.

Unravel a silver or copper scouring pad and press in little pink and red sequin stars. You might want to use dried flowers or little shells instead of sequins. One pad will stretch for about a yard, so you may need a few to decorate a tree.

Here is a way to put Styrofoam® packing chips to good use. Spray them gold and silver and thread them together in an interesting pattern, then loop the garland around your tree for a spectacular effect.

For a softer look, sew together a length of golden ribbon bows. You can sew little glass beads between the bows.

Chinese lanterns make a colorful garland. String the lanterns together with thin copper wire or nylon string, threading shells and beads in between each lantern.

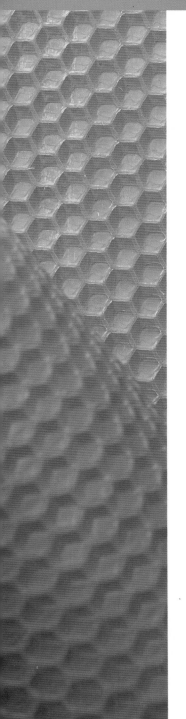

CANDLES

PRACTICAL PROJECTS

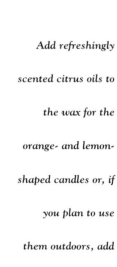

FRUIT BASKET

Rosy apples and ripe pears, tangy oranges and lemons and luscious-looking bunches of grapes – this cheerful candle collection is made using flexible molds you can buy in craft shops.

Make these fruit-shaped candles in fantasy or realistic colors, and if you wish, use acrylic paints to add characteristic color variations. For instance, a patch of rosy red paint, smudged at the edges, turns a sour-looking apple into one that is far more appealing.

When the wax has hardened and the paint is thoroughly dry, polish the fruit pieces using a soft cloth and a few drops of vegetable oil.

Display these lovely fruit candles in a basket lined with contrasting green leaves in a fruit bowl or on a flat dish, piled high in pyramid fashion. When the lights are low, issue a friendly warning to guests – do not attempt to eat the decorations!

Add refreshingly scented citrus oils to the wax for the orange- and lemon-shaped candles or, if you plan to use them outdoors, add citronella oil to keep the bugs away.

SWEET LAVENDER

These dark lavender-colored candles have the sweetest scents of all —

the fragrance of dried lavender flowers blended with the wax. Light one

to give off a subtle aroma in the living room or a romantic aura in

the bedroom.

To make these scented candles, lightly crush dried lavender flowers with a pestle and mortar, or beat them gently with one end of a rolling pin. Be careful not to crush the lavender flowers to a fine powder. Use a blend of blue and red dyes, or a deep violet dye, to color the wax. First, let a little set on a cold saucer to check that you like the shade. To make the darker block candle shown here, pour the melted wax into the prepared square mold; when it is on the point of setting, sprinkle on the crushed lavender flowers. Use a thin wooden stick or a metal skewer to stir them in and distribute them evenly throughout the wax. For a lighter, less dense effect, whisk the melted colored wax with a whisk or an electric mixer. Pour the frothy wax into the prepared mold and, just before it sets, stir in the lavender flowers.

These dinner candles in various colors from pale lavender blue to deep mulberry are scented with lavender oil. They can be displayed in elegant silver or crystal holders, or for a romantic effect, clustered together and tied with gossamer ribbon.

ICE COOL

These highly textured candles are bubbly on the surface and randomly pitted with holes. They are made by a quick-and-easy, fun technique that is applied physics in its lightest form!

To make these "ice candles," insert a slender candle or a taper into a rigid mold of any size or shape. Thread the exposed end of the candle wick through the hole in the mold (do not seal it with mold seal) and stand the mold in a bowl or dish. Then pack the mold with crushed ice or chunks of solid ice. The more ice you use and the larger the chunks, the larger the holes in the candle will be. Now melt, then pour on some melted wax. As it cools, the wax forms a thin skin around the pieces of ice, which will determine the texture of the candle. And as the ice melts and the water runs out of the hole in the base of the mold, it will leave its mark behind – a random pattern of holes in the finished candle.

Children especially like to experiment with this type of candlemaking. They are fascinated to watch the transformation as melted wax and solid ice are changed into solid wax and liquid water. Where young children are concerned, be sure to supervise when the melted wax is poured.

MOSAIC PATTERNS

Pink and blue, orange and violet, yellow and green — color them as you will. These mosaic

candles are made by a simple technique suitable for use in any rigid mold.

To make mosaic candles, thread the wick in the mold in the usual way and seal the hole. Then pack the mold with random chunks of colored wax, pressing them as close as possible against the sides so that the colors will be seen at their brightest.

For the mosaic effect, you can use chunks of wax in a single color or in a combination of two or more colors. You can even use leftover candle ends in this delightfully thrifty way. (To avoid a criss-cross confusion of wicks as the mosaic candle burns down, pull out and discard short pieces of wick in used candle ends.)

Pour on melted white wax to fill in all the spaces and tap the mold sharply on the working surface to settle the wax. Pour on

more wax until the surface is level.

If you are color coordinating candles to match your furnishings or a table theme, remember that the coating of clear wax will dilute the color of the candle chunks inside.

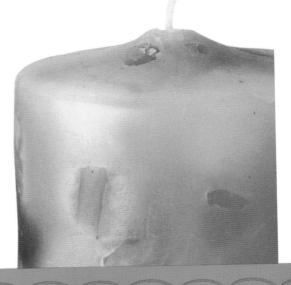

PERFECT CATCH

Make a school of colorful fish-shaped candles to decorate the table for

a poolside party, or create a miniature pond of floating fish candles as

an indoor table centerpiece.

These fish candles can be made in small metal molds, sold in kitchen shops to shape fish mousses or molded gelatin. Or you could shape your own molds using a double thickness of heavy-duty aluminum foil. The candles shown here are about 5 inches long.

To evoke the atmosphere of a brilliant school of tropical fish, make your collection as colorful and exotic as you please. It is a good idea to mold one fish candle each time you are coloring wax for another project.

Brush the molds lightly with vegetable oil for easy release and tip out the shapes when the wax has hardened. Dip a length of wick into melted wax to stiffen it, pierce two holes in each fish shape with a heated metal skewer and insert short pieces of wick into the holes. To add a realistic shimmer to the exotic fish shapes, brush the candle surface all over with a gold metallic acrylic paint.

FALL LEAVES

The fallen leaves of early autumn gathered from the forests and the herb garden can all be arranged

to embellish plain candles that you buy or make yourself. It is a delightful way to add a seasonal note

to your table decorations.

Gather a selection of shapely and colorful leaves and press them between sheets of paper toweling under heavy pressure. Once they are dry, you will have a wealth of decorative materials to enhance plain candles of all shapes and sizes – thick pillar candles, slender dinner candles, or short, squat candles.

Sort through your pressed leaves and grade them according to size. Arrange a selection of leaves around the candle and adjust them into a pleasing pattern. For example, you might like to position a cluster of

golden maple leaves to look as if they are floating down from the tree, or position purple-tinted chervil leaves so that each one is seen in stark silhouette.

Once you have arranged the leaves, run a thin line of melted clear glue around the edges and along the stems, and press them in place. Hold a piece of paper over the leaves to help press down the edges without damaging them.

With the light of
the candle behind
them, the leaves are
seen in all their
intricate detail.

STRAIGHT FROM THE HIVE

Shape warm beeswax in your hands as if it were clay, or melt it and pour it into flexible molds. Either way, it can fire your imagination and help you come up with a honey of an idea for candles with flair.

If you or the children have mastered the art of clay modeling then you have the skill you need at your fingertips to shape and model beeswax.

You may be able to buy beeswax from a local beekeeper. Or you can save ends of old beeswax candles, unroll them to remove the wicks and melt them in a double boiler or in a bowl placed over a pan of just simmering water.

When the wax has cooled, but is still pliable, shape it into hives, domes,

trees, animal figures, or whatever you wish. Push a fine skewer into the wax while it is still soft and insert a length of wick that has been dipped in melted wax. Hive shapes can be made from a flexible mold or else modeled by hand. First mold the dome shape of a bee hive, then model pli-able wax into a long thin roll. Coil this around the dome, pressing it gently onto the surface, and make textural markings with a knife. Shape the bees with your fingers and press them onto the hive.

Molds in the characteristic beeswax shape – the flat hexagon – can be bought in some health food stores or made from a double thickness of heavy-duty aluminum foil. Press a corn cob onto the soft wax to give it the identifiable pattern, then make a bee for the top. The ones shown here, highlighted with gold acrylic paint, are reminiscent of the "golden bee" pendant found at ancient Malia, in Crete.

UNDERSEA EXPLORATION

For an exciting design concept, explore the possibility of setting plain and

colored candle wax in shells of all kinds. The texture contrasts are terrific.

Sort through any shells you have, select those with the deepest cavities and fill them with candlewax. This is a practical and decorative form of recycling.

Fish restaurateurs often give you their empty oyster shells, just for the asking. Wash, scrub and thoroughly dry them, then pick out those that are most suitable to hold a candle. Some halves may be almost flat and would hold very little wax; other shells may have deep hollows that would accommodate a long-burning candle.

The pale pearly colors of shells perfectly complement the soft glow of the candle. You might prefer to color the wax a deep sea blue to add a marine look to your table setting, or perhaps leave the wax uncolored and virtually indistinguishable from the interior of the shell.

To make shell candles, cut short pieces of wick, stick each one to the inside of a shell with a dab of tacky modeling clay and secure the wick vertically. A wooden toothpick is ideal for this. Stand the shells in a dish of sand or rice to keep them level, then pour in the melted wax and allow it to set.

Deep, dark blue

wax inspires an

undersea theme

that is enlarged by

adding seaweed,

driftwood,

and a variety

of shells.

CHRISTMAS-TREE COPSE

Arrange a forest of Christmas-tree candles with all the beauty and mystery of the woods in winter.

There is nothing new about Christmas trees and flickering candles; or is there? These tree-shaped candles in glittering green and gold have added candle-power provided by the slender tapers.

You can buy these shiny bright tree-shaped candles or make them yourself using cookie cutters (see pages 38–39). Use a hand drill with a small gauge drill bit to bore vertical holes in each layer of branches, or

pierce the holes with several applications of a fine metal skewer heated over a candle flame. Cut short pieces of narrow tapers about 5 inches long and insert them into the holes. Because the tapers have a short burning time, reserve them for the highlight of a special occasion. Use them when bringing the Christmas pudding, wreathed in flaming brandy, to the dining table or to draw attention to one of your most spectacular desserts.

You can buy flexible tree-shaped molds to make candles of a completely different character. The frosty green tree shown here was made by mixing together green and pearly white candle dyes and adding to the melted wax.

IVY TRAILS

Transform a trio of chunky tumblers into

candle holders for a patio party. All it

takes is a handful of ivy leaves and a

few twists of raffia.

Place one ivy-trailed candleholder beside each setting at the table; arrange several in a cluster to provide light as dusk falls, or position a row of them along a balcony or around a porch as territorial markers. Positioned as you wish, these novel holders will be the shining light at any party.

To make the ivy-leaf holders, select leaves that are of similar size and shape. Position them around the tumblers to check that they fit, then stick them in place with clear quick-setting glue. Braid or twist together several strands of raffia and tie them around the tumbler.

As an alternative, but with a similar theme, twist long strands of small-leaved ivy around the tumblers and secure them discreetly with short pieces of very fine silver wire.

Place a small candle in each holder. You could add a little glamor by using a golden ball-shaped candle.

Whether you dream of the glory of days gone by or simply want to create an effect for a special occasion, these candles have an intriguing aura of history.

ANCIENT LIGHTS

It is easy to imagine candles like these – painted in deep,

rich tones and tinged with just a hint of gold – casting their

flickering shadows onto old stone walls and medieval manu-

scripts. The effect is reassuringly easy to achieve.

The antique-looking candles are molded in clear wax and painted with watercolor paints mixed with an added ingredient – green dishwashing liquid – to give the surface of the candles a raised and textured finish.

To achieve this effect, mix the watercolor on a palette or a small dish until it is the color you want. Dilute the paint with a couple of drops of liquid detergent and dab it onto the surface of the candle. A small, flat-ended stippling brush is most suitable for this technique.

Let the paint dry, then spray the surface of the candle evenly with artist's fixative. When this sealant has dried, use a fine-tipped camel-hair brush or any similar type of brush to drizzle on thin wavy lines of gold metallic acrylic paint. Let the paint dry thoroughly before picking up the candle.

Deep, dark colors such as burgundy, midnight blue, and forest green are most effective for these candles, which imitate the deep rich tones and glittering threads of medieval tapestries and silks.

BLACK & GOLD

Black and gold candles, black tableware inlaid with mother-of-pearl, and golden accessories bring glamor to the table.

A tracery of golden ivy leaves painted around slender black dinner candles creates an elegant look that is surprisingly easy to achieve.

You may decide to buy gold-painted candles as the focal point of your table setting. Or, at a fraction of the cost, you may prefer to decorate plain candles as described here.

Gold metallic acrylic paint is the most tenacious medium to use on the hard shiny surface of candlewax. It is possible to apply the paint through a stencil, dabbing it on with a small stippling brush, but it is not easy to lift off the stencil without causing the edges to smear.

With very little practice, even the least accomplished artist is likely to achieve a neater finish by painting on the leaves – a reassuringly simple, near-triangular shape – with a fine-tipped camel-hair or similar paint brush. Practice painting the leaf shapes on a piece of paper, then paint them at random, to wind around the candles. When the paint is dry, add a second coat if necessary.

AN INTERESTING TWIST

Layer upon layer of colored wax is revealed in these sculptured candles as they

are carved into twists and folds, bows and spirals.

The craft of hand carving these lovely candles, a tradition in parts of the United States and Northern Europe, is presently enjoying a popular revival on both sides of the Atlantic.

Each candle is built up around a star-shaped core of uncolored wax and stearin set in a ready-made metal mold. The core candle is then dipped into a series of dye vats, each one containing melted wax of a different color. It is the skill of blending the various colors, at least as much as the skill of carving the candle, that creates these traditional works of art.

After the final color-dipping – there may be as many as thirty applications – suspend the candle on a rod while you carve the warm and

pliable outer wax into thin slivers. This is not a craft for tentative people because, depending on the humidity and temperature of the room, there may be only five minutes in which to shape the wax.

Trim the wick before lighting it, tip away any melted wax that forms in the well of the candle and limit each burning session to about one-and-a-half hours for small candles and about three hours for large ones.

After many hours of burning, when you are left with just a decorative and hollow candle shell, insert a smaller, scented household or votive candle into the shell, and

enjoy the intricacy of the carved candle all over again.

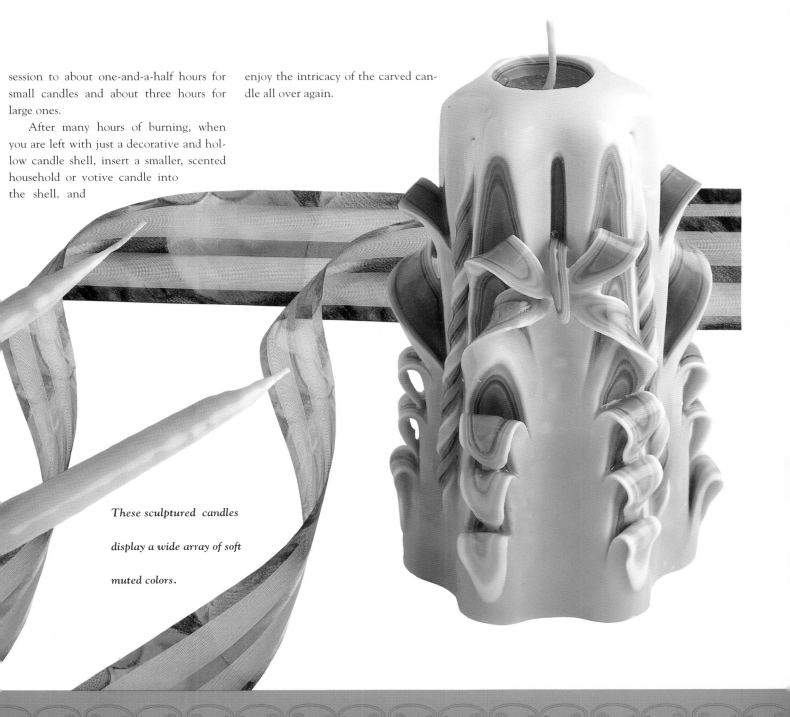

These sculptured candles

display a wide array of soft

muted colors.

WREATHS

PRACTICAL PROJECTS

NARCISSUS & IVY WREATH

Paper white narcissus, one of the first flowers of spring, appears in even the

most inclement weather to herald the beginning of the gardening season.

An ivy wreath

sprinkled with

delicate white

flowers brings

a touch of spring

into the house.

A simple wreath made from bunches of these delicate white flowers looks particularly fresh when offset by contrasting dark green ivy leaves.

Prepare the base for this wreath by placing handfuls of damp sphagnum moss, which have been soaked in water for a few hours beforehand, around a small wire frame. Use garden twine to hold the moss in place (see Basic Techniques). Cut the ends of the narcissus stems diagonally.

Working in one direction, place the ivy leaves and narcissi on the frame so that they overlap and their stems push lightly into the damp moss. Bend small pieces of stub wire into U shapes and push them over the stems through the moss to the back of the wreath to hold everything firmly in place.

HYACINTH WREATH

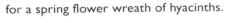

Blue and white is a fresh and vibrant color combination

for a spring flower wreath of hyacinths.

This wreath calls for the same type of moss-covered wire frame as the one used for the narcissus and ivy wreath. Push short sprigs of laurustinus into the moss, working around the circle in the same direction to cover the base and provide a lush background for the flowers. Bend short pieces of stub wire into U shapes and push them over the stems to hold the laurustinus in place.

Before adding the flowers, cut the stems diagonally. Arrange the blue hyacinths around the wreath among the laurustinus. Push the stems into the moss and hold them in place with wire. Follow the same procedure for the white hyacinths, dotting them around the circle among the foliage and blue hyacinths.

To keep your fresh flower wreaths looking good for as long as possible, spray the flowers, foliage and moss base regularly with water.

The exquisite-looking wreath shown here has an added bonus – the sweet scent of hyacinths.

This woodland egg wreath is decorated with small speckled quail eggs. Make sure that the eggs have been kept at room temperature for several hours beforehand. Pierce both ends of the egg with a sharp needle, then push the needle carefully through the hole to break up the egg inside. Holding the egg over a dish, gently blow out the yolk and white. Wash out each blown egg with a disinfectant, rinse it well and let dry. Make platforms for the eggs to sit on by bending the ends of stub wires into small flat loops. Glue the quail eggs securely onto the wire platforms.

To make the wreath, bind a wire frame with damp sphagnum moss in the usual way (see Basic Techniques). Cover the top side of the base with large pieces of carpet moss and hold them in place with short U-shaped pieces of wire pushed down into the moss around the edges. Arrange small bunches of forget-me-nots around the

WOODLAND EGG WREATH

Deep green carpet moss makes a sumptuous base for a woodland

wreath that incorporates catkins and pretty speckled quail eggs.

circle; push the stems into the moss and pin them in position with wires. Add some catkins, pushing the stems into the moss. Finally, add dried mushrooms and quail eggs and wire them in place. Yellow and white checked bows complete this delightful woodland design.

FOIL-WRAPPED CANDY WREATH

Stunning wreaths can be made from everyday materials.

Colorful foil-wrapped candies combined with tiny fluted baking cups make an interesting decorative wreath that resembles Mexican folk art.

The base for this wreath is a standard wire frame that has been pressed and flattened slightly to reduce the angle of the sides. The frame is then covered with metallic cardboard. In order to shape the cardboard to fit the frame, roll the frame slowly over the cardboard and mark the inside and outside edges with a pencil as you go. This makes it easier to fit the cardboard onto the frame. Tie it onto the frame with ribbon slotted through slits cut along the inner and outer edges of the cardboard.

Arrange oval and round fluted baking cups around the circle and fasten them in place with a glue gun. Glue a candy inside each baking cup. Glue longer, thin-shaped candies to fill the gaps between the baking cups. Tie short pieces of cord around the long thin candies and thread the cord through holes made with an awl in the cardboard. Tie the cord into knots and trim the ends.

CARDBOARD WREATH

Wreaths made from the simplest materials can give

surprisingly stylish results.

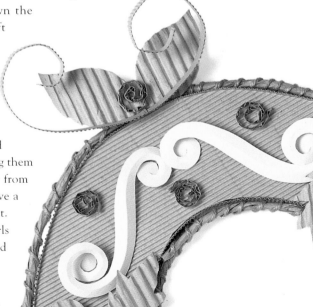

This oval wreath is decorated with scrolls made from smooth cardboard and acanthus leaves made from chunky corrugated cardboard. The colors have been kept simple – a combination of white and natural – and the different textures have been deliberately placed side by side. The wreath is so elegant it could double as a frame for a picture or mirror. It would also look good sprayed gold, enhancing the classical style of the design.

To make the oval wreath base, first draw a pattern on paper. For an even shape, start by drawing a quarter of the oval onto a piece of paper folded into quarters, then transpose this quarter onto the other three parts. Copy the oval pattern on

a piece of fine corrugated cardboard, then cut it out. Cut thin strips of cardboard and stick them in place around the inner and outer edges of the oval to give it depth.

Cut the scrolls out of smooth white cardboard and score them freehand on the front, applying light pressure down the middle of the scrolls with a craft knife. Bend the scrolls along the scoring to give them faceted sides. Cut the acanthus leaf shapes out of thick corrugated cardboard and then arrange them with the scrolls onto the oval base. Glue the scrolls and leaves in place, allowing them to twist and lift away from the base in places to give a three-dimensional effect.

Glue some small curls of rolled-up corrugated

cardboard into the spaces between the shapes. Finish the inner and outer side edges by gluing on rolled-up cardboard or paper raffia bound with string. Place an acanthus leaf with curled bands and a small curl made from corrugated cardboard at the top of the wreath to complete the design.

A spicy wreath makes a pleasant and practical decoration for your kitchen. The choice of decorative spices is a matter of personal taste.

CHILE & PEPPERCORN WREATH

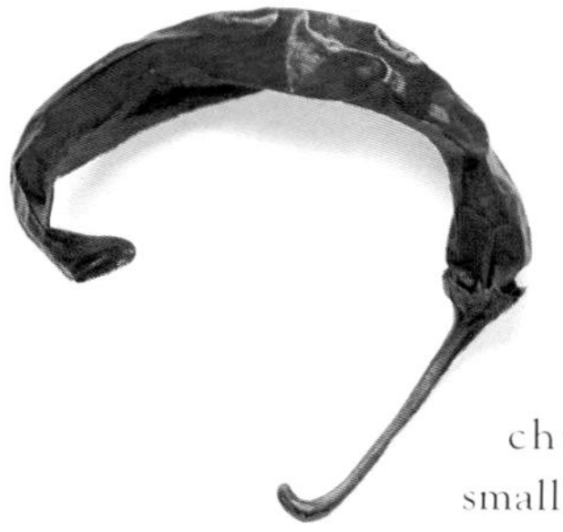

A ring of dried chile peppers and small bunches of pink peppercorns provide interesting shapes and colors for this hot spicy wreath, which would look good in any country kitchen. Try adding more spices to make practical and aromatic variations; whole garlic heads, and small cheesecloth bags of cloves, coriander seeds and cardamom pods are ideal.

The wreath shown here uses a ready-made natural-colored wreath base with overlapping corn husks. It is very simple but provides plenty of interest and texture for this spicy display.

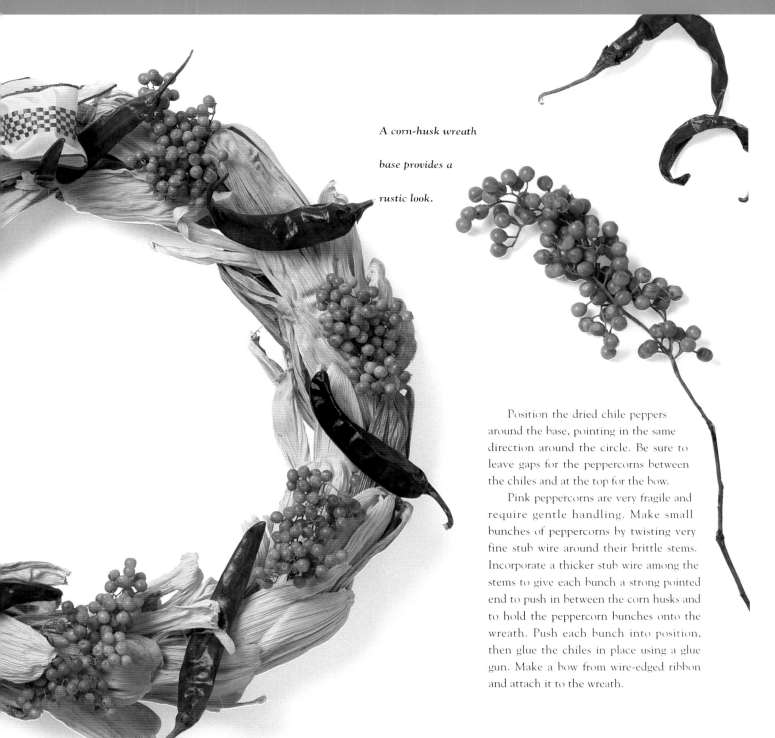

A corn-husk wreath

base provides a

rustic look.

Position the dried chile peppers around the base, pointing in the same direction around the circle. Be sure to leave gaps for the peppercorns between the chiles and at the top for the bow.

Pink peppercorns are very fragile and require gentle handling. Make small bunches of peppercorns by twisting very fine stub wire around their brittle stems. Incorporate a thicker stub wire among the stems to give each bunch a strong pointed end to push in between the corn husks and to hold the peppercorn bunches onto the wreath. Push each bunch into position, then glue the chiles in place using a glue gun. Make a bow from wire-edged ribbon and attach it to the wreath.

Shells, with their intricate shapes and patterns make a lovely display. Dried seaweed, and bits of driftwood complete the maritime theme.

A wreath frame made of pale twigs gives a natural windswept and sun-bleached look to this shell wreath. Wind several long strands of raffia around the base. Start by tying the raffia around one strand of wood on the back of the twig base and finish by securing the ends and trimming away any excess, but without making it too neat.

SHELL WREATH

A wreath made of seashells and other bits and pieces

that have washed ashore helps to keep alive

those pleasant memories of trips to the

beach on warm summer days.

Arrange shells, dried seaweed, starfish and small pieces of driftwood around the wreath base in groups, with spaces between for the base to show through. Glue them in place using a glue gun. A piece of driftwood, bound and tied with strands of raffia, is wired at the top of the wreath. The ends of the raffia are allowed to curl and dangle down naturally into the center of the ring.

CHILD'S FOLK ART WREATH

For a child's wreath with folk art charm, simply use up

scraps of homespun checkered fabrics and striped

ticking fabric. This makes an ideal decoration

for a child's bedroom.

The padded animal shapes can be permanently stitched to the base or fastened on with Velcro so they can be removed and played with as toys.

Use a narrow twig base and wrap it with a bias-cut strip of ticking fabric 1½ inches wide. Make the strip by stitching together shorter pieces of fabric. When the base is covered, stitch the strip in place at the back of the base.

Make paper patterns of simple animal shapes – a puppy, a rabbit, an elephant, and a teddy bear – with a small seam allowance around each one. Using these patterns, cut the animal shapes out of scraps of brightly colored checkered fabrics; allow two pieces for each animal. With right sides of the fabric together, stitch each pair of shapes around the edges, leaving a hole for the padding. Cut the seam allowances along the curves before turning right side out. Stuff the animals lightly with a washable polyester padding, which helps to soften the shapes. When padded, sew up the hole. Stitch a tiny bow to the neck of each animal.

Place the animals around the wreath and fasten them in place with small pieces of Velcro® stitched to the backs of each of them and in corresponding positions on the wreath. Alternatively, stitch the animals directly onto the base.

The ingredients for a kitchen wreath can be removed when needed and new herbs and spices added to fill in the bare spots. Use a combination of herbs, choosing a good mix of colors and textures; the wreath shown here uses bay leaves, rosemary, thyme and purple sage.

Cover a wire frame with damp moss and bind in place with twine (see Basic Techniques). Trim herbs with woody stems into 4 inch pieces, cutting the stems diagonally so that the ends are pointed. Gather the softer stemmed varieties, such as sage and thyme, into small bunches, using florist's wire with an end left pointing out for attaching to the wreath.

Arrange the herbs around the moss base so that they face in one direction all the way around. Push the pointed stems directly into the moss, and push the wires on the bunches through to the back of the frame and wind around to secure. Wire a bow to the wreath to finish.

This rich green wreath can be made with your favorite herbs from the garden.

KITCHEN HERB WREATH

A wreath made from fresh herbs and hung near the stove makes a useful,

aromatic decoration for the kitchen. It will continue to

look good as it dries out naturally.

COTTAGE GARDEN WREATH

Cottage garden flowers perfectly capture the spirit of midsummer, and many of

these blooms can easily be dried for displaying when the season is over.

Always pick the flowers on a clear sunny morning, after the dew has evaporated, choosing well-shaped and blemish-free heads that are not too open. Find a warm place with good ventilation for drying. Hang the flowers upside-down to dry in small bunches; keeping them away from bright light helps to retain their rich colors. This summer wreath is made from a sumptuous mixture of pink and blue flowers – lavender, peonies, love-lies-bleeding, rose-buds, globe thistle, lark-spur, and love-in-a-mist – with eucalyptus and sage leaves for foliage.

A circle of dry florist's foam makes an ideal firm base for a dry flower wreath. Cut the eucalyptus into short pieces and push them into the foam, working in one direction around the wreath and allowing some of the leaves to break out naturally around the edges of the frame. Carefully wire the sage and lavender into small bunches with fine florist's wire. Push the bundles in between the eucalyptus stems.

Next, push the large peony heads and the remaining blooms into position, placing them at random to fill in all the gaps for a dense effect. Wire a bow to the top of the wreath to finish.

VEGETABLE WREATH

A crop of miniature vegetables, freshly picked from the kitchen garden, can be turned into a delightful wreath.

These everyday foods take on an ornamental quality when arranged to emphasize their subtle coloring and markings. Baby artichokes, eggplants, and asparagus can also be included in this vegetable wreath, as well as pink turnips, tiny ears of corn, and even a small cabbage or cauliflower.

All the vegetables must be wired for attaching to the wreath (see Basic Techniques). Push pieces of stub wire through the vegetables, then twist together leaving a long end. Gather smaller items such as radishes and Brussels sprouts into bunches and asparagus spears into bundles with a few twists of fine wire. Cover the wire with twine or raffia and tie the ends in a knot. Wrap a wire frame with some damp sphagnum moss and bind it with twine (see Basic Techniques). Cover the frame with a foliage background of laurustinus interspersed with sprigs of rosemary. Push the stems into the moss, working in one direction around the ring.

Arrange the vegetables in groups among the foliage, pushing the wires through the moss to the back and twisting the ends a couple of times around the frame. A bow provides a finishing detail.

Vegetables in various shapes, sizes, and colors have been arranged in groups.

Cabbage leaves add beautifully subtle textures to a wreath.

ROSE WREATH

A continuous ring of fresh roses interspersed with bits of

foliage celebrates summer at its best.

For this wreath, old-fashioned garden roses or long-stemmed roses give a softer, more natural look than the hybrid tea roses or floribunda types.

Rosebuds worked onto a single wire frame and allowed to dry and fade naturally result in a long-lasting circlet that has its own special beauty. Alternatively, full-blown roses will give a spectacular but fleeting effect since they are likely to drop their petals as they dry.

Wire each rose by cutting the stem to about one and a half inches and pushing a piece of stub wire horizontally through the base of the flower head. Bend and wind the wire down over the natural stem, to create a false stem. Cover this new flexible stem with florist's tape. Buds and spray roses need to be wired into small bunches.

After wiring all the roses, wind them onto a single-wire base, working in one direction around it and interspersing the flower heads with foliage.

This lovely summer wreath was made with a blend of pink and peach roses.

SACHET WREATH

Lavender sachets that bring their sweet fragrance to the linen closet can also

be used to decorate wreaths that perfume the rest of your home.

The sachets on this wreath were made with small pieces of checkered Madras cotton fabric, which comes in wonderfully mellow color combinations.

Use a plain wooden vine base to give a rustic feel to this sachet wreath. Wind strings of metal leaves (with wire stems and a bright verdigris finish) around the base, then twist and arrange the leaves at different angles around the circle. Other leafy coverings, such as dried stems

of long-leaved eucalyptus, can be used instead, but the overall look should be kept sparse and simple.

For each lavender sachet, cut out a fabric rectangle measuring 6 inches by 5 inches; this includes a half-inch seam allowance. Fold the rectangle in half lengthwise, with the right sides of the fabric facing together, and stitch the open side and bottom edges. Trim the seam allowance and turn the fabric right side out

to make a small bag. Turn the open unfinished edge at the top of the bag to the inside and iron the folded edge flat, making a sachet that is approximately 4 inches deep.

Fill each bag two-thirds full with dried lavender flowers and tie a ribbon around to close up the top. Push a piece of stub wire through the fabric on the back of each sachet; twist the wire around itself to leave a long end. Push the wire through the wreath base to the back and carefully wrap it around one thickness of vine.

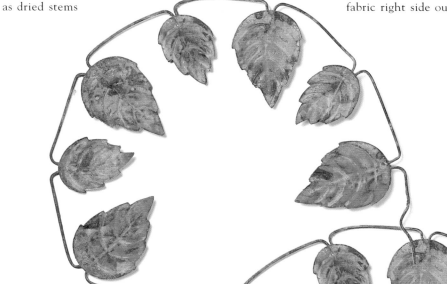

A string of metal

leaves provides

an added touch.

Little sachets of lavender in checkered

Madras fabric give this simple summer

wreath an unmistakable feel of the country.

Choose colors that blend with your

furnishings.

HARVEST SQUARE WREATH

A wreath of golden wheat and other fruits of the field

celebrates the rich bounty of harvest time.

The fall harvest wreath follows the British tradition of the corn dolly, which is a small figure made from dried wheat. Farmers used to make corn dollies to keep the spirit of the harvested field safe throughout the long winter, ready to be released again in the spring.

The square frame is an unusual alternative and could be used to frame a mirror or sit on a shelf. To make the frame, arrange a square of four woody sticks with their ends crossed, then bind the corners with some garden twine. Cover the sticks with sphagnum moss

and bind it on with twine (see Basic Techniques). Allow the moss to dry out thoroughly before decorating.

Wire dried golden wheat into small bundles, leaving a long end of wire. Trim the bundles neatly, then cover the wires with garden twine and tie it into a knot. Arrange the bundles of wheat around the frame, leaving a space at the top, and fasten them to the frame by wrapping the stub wires around the sticks. Wire together a few dried sunflower heads and attach them to the wreath at the top. Create a focal point with a flourish of ribbon in seasonal tones.

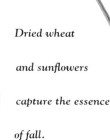

Dried wheat

and sunflowers

capture the essence

of fall.

DRIED FLOWER WREATH

Dried fall fruits and flowers were mixed together to produce this mellow color combination.

Dried flowers,

pods, and seed

heads are featured

in this fall wreath.

Make a foundation for this dried flower wreath by bending supple tree branches (we've used twisted hazel) together into a ring. Extra branches can be added when necessary, but allow the wispy ends to curl outward around the sides of the wreath base.

To dry the hydrangeas, hang them upside-down in a warm place. Covering the flower heads with a paper bag helps to retain their color. Alternatively, leave the hydrangeas in a jug of water until the water has

evaporated. Dry pomegranates by storing them in a warm place until they dry out.

Group dried pomegranates, dried hydrangeas, seed heads, and pods on the base, allowing gaps for the woody base to show through. Push wires through the fruits and flower heads and wind them around the stems. Then fasten the pomegranates and hydrangeas onto the frame. Glue the seed heads and pods in place, using a glue gun. Finally, tie a taffeta ribbon bow and wire it to the bottom of the wreath.

A circle of autumn leaves adorned with larch cones creates

a wreath with a classical feel.

OAK LEAF WREATH

Working with dry, brittle leaves can be extremely tricky and calls for a light and delicate touch.

Prewire each oak leaf by gluing a short piece of fine reel wire to the back of each leaf. Carefully twist one end of the wire a few times around the stem. Then arrange the oak leaves around a wire ring frame, leaving spaces between them. Secure the leaves by winding the other end of each wire around the wreath frame to hold the leaf in position. Cut off any excess wire.

When you have completed the circle of leaves, glue a short piece of fine reel wire near the base of each larch cone and attach to the wreath. Secure everything in place with small blobs of glue over the wires on the underside of the frame.

BERRY WREATH

Fall brings with it an abundance of richly colored foliage and

branches heavy with fruits and berries.

Decorate a wreath with a fall bouquet of rosehips, brambles, and viburnum gathered from the forests and countryside. Berries and foliage, especially those varieties with leathery leaves, will hold up well in cool conditions for about three weeks. Both berries and leaves will shrink slightly as they dry out, but they should still hold their color. Spraying with water each day will help the wreath to last longer.

To make a berry wreath, bend branches of pyracantha around a vine base, with the leaves and bunches of berries facing the front. Secure the branches with garden raffia. Add other foliage with berries to fill out the wreath and add color and texture. Cut stems of eucalyptus with frothy pinkish fruits into short sprays, push them in among the pyracantha, and fasten in place with wires twisted around the base. Add bunches of spindle berries and spiky stems of myrtle.

Another method of making a berry wreath is to cut a wreath out of thin plywood. Layer branches of foliage and berries around the base so they all face in one direction with the leaves of each branch covering the stems of the branch next to it. Staple the branches to the base with a staple gun. Attach a picture hook on the back of the frame to hang the wreath.

Rosy red berries set against a glossy green background give a feeling of warmth and cheer to this garland of leathery leaves.

A pretty lavender wreath draped casually over a lampshade is a lovely sight and an unusual way to display a flower arrangement.

A simple wreath made from aromatic lavender flowers is an elegant way to decorate a lampshade. A single wire ring used for making lampshades is ideal for the wreath frame. Choose a size that will sit comfortably one half to one third of the way down your lampshade. Please remember that dried material is flammable so the wreath should not be left for long periods when the lamp is switched on.

Gather together small bunches of dried lavender on long stems; twist fine reel wire a few times around the stems just below the flower heads, leaving a long end of wire. Trim all the stems to make bunches that are approximately 4 inches in length. Working around the outer edge of the ring frame, bind the lavender bunches onto the frame one by one with each bunch facing the same direction and the flowers overlapping the stems of the bunch next to it. When the wreath is completely covered, tie a piece of ribbon around it, making a bow that has long trailing ends.

LAVENDER LAMPSHADE WREATH

The color and sweet fragrance of lavender has a timeless appeal.

A profusion of a single type of flower, such as lavender, makes a beautifully simple wreath.

Citrus fruits add their bright colorings and distinctive scent

to a simple wreath of glossy green bay leaves.

DRIED CITRUS WREATH

Gather fresh bay leaves into bunches and wire the stems together with fine reel wire. Bind the bunches onto a twig base by wrapping natural raffia over the stems. Point all the bay leaf bunches the same direction and place each bunch with the leaves over-lapping the stems of the previous bunch. When the wreath is completely clad with bay leaves, thread dried orange slices into groups of five or six on pieces of raffia with the ends brought together and tied into bows. Fasten these circles onto the wreath with wire. Wire each lime with two stub wires on each fruit (see Basic Techniques) and fasten in place by twisting the wires around the back of the twig base. Finish off the wreath with a bow made from several strands of raffia.

Dried orange slices can be bought from specialist suppliers, or you can dry them yourself by baking them slowly in the oven at a low temperature until they are hard. Small lemons and kumquats wired into bunches would make attractive and colorful additions.

Bay leaves make

a lush base for

orange slices and

small limes.

STAR WREATH

Decorating the door with a Christmas wreath follows in a tradition that began

with the ancient Romans, who exchanged evergreen branches bent into rings to

symbolize good health.

This festive green and white star-shaped wreath of eucalyptus, broom, and larch is a modern variation on the traditional ring of evergreen branches.

Make the five-pointed star frame from three wire coat hangers. Measure down from the point on each side of the hanger and cut to the same length using wire cutters. Arrange these wire points to form the star shape, with the wire ends bent back approximately 1 inch, at an angle, so that

each end overlaps the next one, forming the star's inside corners. Glue each overlap and bind with wire to hold it firmly together.

Cover the star frame with sphagnum moss bound on with twine (see Basic Techniques). Remember, when making a single wire frame like this, to keep the weight as light as possible at this stage so that the weight of the finished wreath does not pull the frame out of shape.

The green and

white theme of this

star wreath reflects

the subdued colors

of winter.

Cut fine-leaved eucalyptus into short pieces with pointed ends that are easy to push into the moss frame. Place white broom, with stems cut short, in among the eucalyptus, then secure them in place with small U-shaped pieces of stub wire, twisted together at the back of the frame. Add short twigs of larch and wire them in place. A green bow, attached with wire, adds a nice finishing touch.

As an alternative, decorate your star wreath with white Christmas roses. Their waxy flowers will stay fresh for quite some time. Clusters of cranberries nestled in among the dark green foliage would provide a cheerful color contrast. The red berries could be highlighted with a red bow.

ACKNOWLEDGEMENTS

The Publisher would like to thank the following for their contributions to this book:

Fenella Brown for her help in supplying parcels, ornaments, bows and garlands for many of the projects photographed.

Heini Schneebeli for his photographs.

Candles were supplied by -
Price's Patent Candle Co. London, England
Easy-Bee Candles, Gloucestershire, England
The Hand-Crafted Candle Company, Suffolk, England

Emma Hardy for all her help in making the wreaths and Caroline Alexander of the Hop Shop in Kent, England, for supplying dried flowers.